Original title:
Floral Fables

Copyright © 2025 Creative Arts Management OÜ
All rights reserved.

Author: Evan Hawthorne
ISBN HARDBACK: 978-1-80566-631-8
ISBN PAPERBACK: 978-1-80566-916-6

The Scent of Sudden Sunshine

In the garden, daisies dance,
Chasing shadows with a prance.
Bees in bow ties buzz around,
While tulips wear their gowns profound.

A rose told jokes with petals wide,
The sun laughed loud, it can't abide.
Lilacs blushed at every pun,
As violets strutted, just for fun.

Dandelions joined the jest,
With little hats, they felt the best.
A tulip said, "I can't take this,
My beauty's fading in this bliss!"

But laughter thrived where colors bloomed,
In a world where giggles zoomed.
Sunshine's scent, a tickling breeze,
Where each flower aims to please.

Butterflies and Blossoms in Harmony

Butterflies in polka dots,
Flutter 'round the blooming pots.
Petals giggle, colors bright,
Joking with the bees in flight.

A daffodil told quite the tale,
Of its cousin lost in a gale.
"Worry not!" a lilac cried,
"Just wear a hat and take a ride!"

A bumblebee named Barry flew,
Tripped on blooms of glowing hue.
He tumbled down, but laughed with glee,
"Just practicing my acrobatic spree!"

In this world of fluttering fun,
Every bloom shines, none a shun.
Together they laugh, sing, and dance,
In nature's wild and wacky romance.

The Voices of the Blossoms

On sunny days, the daisies chat,
They gossip sweetly, 'What a hat!'
The roses laugh, 'We're bold and bright!',
While violets giggle in purple light.

The sunflowers sway, they're always right,
Saying, 'Follow us, it's quite a sight!'
The tulips tease, 'We're tall and neat,'
While daisies dance on little feet.

Legends of the Lotus

A lotus sighed, 'I'm quite the queen!',
'The murky pond is where I've been.'
The frogs croaked back, 'You're just a tease,
With your pretty petals, that sway in breeze.'

They spun tall tales of dreams so grand,
How a lotus ruled a happy land.
But all agreed in playful tone,
The best of fun is when they're grown.

Canvas of Colors in Bloom

In gardens bright, a palette spills,
Colors clash with laughter and thrills.
Yellow daisies wink at red,
While bluebells dance, their faces spread.

A splash of green, a dash of pink,
A rainbow jokes, 'Come here and think!'
The butterflies flap, 'What a sight!'
As bees bump heads in sheer delight.

Grace of the Geranium

The geranium sways with flair and style,
It twirls around, making flowers smile.
It tells the tales of windy days,
And how it danced in sunlit rays.

With petals bright, it plays the fool,
Saying, 'I'm the coolest in the school!'
The other plants laugh, they agree,
That grace and jokes are all for free.

The Enchanted Arbor's Tale

In a grove where giggles bloom,
Trees wear hats, dispelling gloom.
Squirrels dance with floppy shoes,
Telling stories 'neath the hues.

Mushrooms laugh, tickling the air,
While daisies gossip without a care.
A rabbit spins in joyous glee,
Making friends with bumblebees.

With each twist of every vine,
Petals whisper tales divine.
The moonlight winks, the stars agree,
In this tree, all are carefree!

So if you wander near this place,
Join the fun, embrace the chase.
For under branches, laughter sways,
In the arbored dance of days.

Garden of Forgotten Chants

In a garden where whispers play,
Flowers laugh and frogs croon sway.
Butterflies tell jokes so bright,
While snails slide by with sheer delight.

Vines twist into silly shapes,
Creating hats for all the apes.
Petunias wave as if to tease,
Bees hum tunes like summer breeze.

A playful breeze begins to sing,
Joking with the blooming spring.
And every thorn has tales to spin,
Of laughter found in joy within.

So come and stroll where flowers flip,
And secrets bloom from every tip.
In this garden, you'll find the chance,
To dance along with whispers' dance.

The Poetry of Thorned Roses

In a patch where roses prance,
Thorns wear laughter, join the dance.
Petals wink with colors bright,
As the sunsets paint the night.

Each bud has jokes that bloom and spin,
Enticing butterflies to join in.
A rose declares with cheeky flair,
"Thorns are just nature's way to pair!"

Chasing bees with words in flow,
While ladybugs steal the show.
Nature's humor, sharp and sweet,
Makes the garden feel complete.

So tread lightly, enjoy the tease,
Amongst the blooms, you're sure to freeze.
For in this patch of prickly prose,
Laughter blossoms from thorned roses.

Sprite of the Lilac Breeze

A sprite flits by on lilac wings,
Spreading laughter and silly things.
With petals bright and eyes that twinkle,
She sprinkles fun in every wrinkle.

The tall grass giggles at her dance,
As dandelions join in the chance.
"Catch me if you can!" she sings,
While butterflies sport funny rings.

A breeze whooshes, tickling leaves,
As daisies plot a prank that deceives.
Each flower joins her wild spree,
Creating joy for all to see.

So if you sense a lilac whiff,
Join the fun, don't be a stiff.
For the sprite brings joy with ease,
In the whispers of the lilac breeze.

Fragrant Adventures in the Meadow

In the meadow, flowers dance,
Bees in pajamas, what a chance!
Daisies giggle, while they sway,
Sending all the clouds away.

Buttercups wear crowns so bright,
Claiming kingship with delight.
The grass is itchy, but we laugh,
As ants parade like they own half.

A dandelion takes a leap,
From its throne, it doesn't creep.
With a puff, it shares its dreams,
Turning wishes into memes.

Sunflowers talk about their height,
And challenge roses in a fight.
"I'm the tallest!" shouts the bloom,
While tulips plot with much to groom.

The Sunlit Tapestry of Blooms

Petunias prance in a silly line,
While violets sip their sun-taste wine.
Snapdragons laugh with a cheeky grin,
As sunbeams tickle their leafy skin.

Lavender hums a jazzy tune,
Swaying lightly beneath the moon.
Poppies act like they own the stage,
Turning every frown to a giggle page.

Daffodils wobble on tiny stems,
Play hide and seek with all the gems.
The daisies roll on the green grass,
Making butterflies stop and gasp.

A wild rose shares a funny tale,
Of how it once tried to catch a snail.
"But he was fast!" it cackles loud,
As petals burst with laughter proud.

Petals on the Wind

Petals float on a careless breeze,
Tickling noses, oh, such tease!
Butterflies chase them in delight,
Wondering where they'll land tonight.

A breeze whispers to a daisy,
"Dance with me! It's getting hazy!"
But daisies, always quite composed,
Respond with grace, no need for posed.

Roses blush at a passing breeze,
Whispering secrets to the trees.
"Did you hear?" snickers minty sprig,
"Last week's bloom forgot its own gig!"

Lavender spins 'round in a whirl,
Joining in with a joyful twirl.
And as they float, they share a grin,
Petals laughing, let the fun begin!

Mythical Blossoms of the Night

In the garden, blooms talk at night,
With fireflies twinkling, oh, what a sight!
Moonflowers giggle, their faces aglow,
As they create shadows that dance and flow.

Lilies whisper old fairy tales,
Of mischievous gnomes who ride on snails.
While night-blooming cacti stretch wide,
Poking fun at the sleeping tide.

Wisteria drapes in a dreamy way,
Pretending it's the night's cabaret.
With jokes that sparkle in moonbeams' light,
They laugh and twirl, such a warm sight.

A petunia claims it's a star,
Dreaming of fame and a gold guitar.
While the others chuckle, oh what a play,
In the night garden, it's a cabaret!

Tales from the Garden of Secrets

In a garden where daisies lie,
The sunflowers gossip, oh my, oh my!
The roses wear hats, so quite grand,
While the violets make a rock band.

Bees wear shades and dance on their toes,
While the mint leaves tease with ticklish woes.
The carrots conspire, plotting a feast,
While the lettuce dreams of becoming a beast.

The tulips giggle, each bloom a delight,
Telling tall tales in the soft moonlight.
The poppies, in red, sing silly refrains,
Oh, the laughter that bubbles like sweet champagne!

So join in the fun, leave your woes at the gate,
For magic awaits while the flowers debate.
In this garden of secrets that never grows old,
Each petal tells stories that never were told.

Chronicles in Full Bloom

Once in a patch where the daisies convene,
The marigolds plot like a comedic scene.
With petals so bright, they play hide and seek,
While the lilacs chuckle, 'Aren't we unique?'

The sunbeams whisper, tickling the breeze,
As the snapdragons tease with a chorus of 'cheese!'
Oh, how the tulips prance in their prime,
Hoping to catch a flutter of rhyme.

In this land where all veggies conspire,
The zucchinis dream of a bright brass choir.
Radishes laugh as they pull at their roots,
While the onions plot in their funky suits.

Each morning unfurls with whimsical cheer,
As the daisies tell tales that we long to hear.
So come and join this hilarious show,
In the chronicles where all flowers glow.

Secrets Beneath the Petal

Beneath the petals, secrets are spun,
With roses declaring, 'We're so much fun!'
The daisies conspire, not shy to be bold,
As pansies share stories of treasure and gold.

The tulips play pranks by hiding their hue,
While daisies giggle at the old morning dew.
With whispers of mischief, the garden does bloom,
Creating a ruckus, like a burst of perfume.

In shadows and sunlight, laughter takes flight,
As the lavender jokes about stars and moonlight.
Witty and wise, they dance in the sun,
In a world where each flower has humor to run.

So peek through the petals, find joy in surprise,
In a garden of secrets where humor never dies.
With each funny tale, let your spirit feel free,
For in bloom's gentle humor, wonders will be.

The Blooming Heart's Confession

Oh heart of a primrose, so bold and so brave,
Confessing to daisies, 'I just want to rave!'
The violets chuckle at tales of great loves,
While the bees buzz around, like clumsy little doves.

'Why be shy?' asks the cheeky red rose,
As sunflowers grin in their bright golden clothes.
With petals aflutter, they dance and they twirl,
In a garden where laughter creates such a whirl.

The orchids throw parties, outrageous and spry,
While blooming with secrets, they let out a sigh.
'Love's like a bloom,' they say with a wink,
'It sometimes falls flat, yet still makes you think!'

So gather your blooms, for confession is key,
In a heart full of laughter, we flourish with glee.
Each petal a promise, each leaf a good time,
In this joyous garden, life's truly a rhyme.

Symphony of the Night Bloom

In the garden where critters play,
Flowers giggle in a humorous way,
A daisy danced with a cheeky grin,
While the moon just chuckled, taking it in.

A rose told jokes that were simply grand,
The tulips clapped, had them planned firsthand,
With petals so bright, they swayed with delight,
As crickets provided the rhythm that night.

The violets snickered, what a parade,
While the poppies pranced, never dismayed,
Each bloom shared laughs, sprightly and free,
Under twinkling stars, just wait and see!

They spun tales of bees and their sticky plight,
Of squirrels playing tricks, oh what a sight!
So if you wander when the moon is aglow,
Join the blooms in the night, let your laughter flow.

A Melody in the Meadow

In the meadow, where laughter's found,
A sunflower joked, all merry and round,
The daisies joined in, with witty retort,
As butterflies twirled, in playful cohort.

A bee buzzed by with a comical sting,
Said, "I'm off to find the sweetest bling!"
The clover chimed in, "You'll need quite a crew,
Maybe even a rose, or two just for you."

The grass sang a tune, off-key but true,
While drooping daisies giggled, not feeling blue,
In every corner, a pun was made,
As petals whispered secrets in the glade.

Together they laughed, in harmony bright,
Creating a symphony, pure delight,
So next time you wander, just take it slow,
Join the meadow's giggles, let your laughter grow!

The Wildflower's Confession

A wildflower stood, in a curious pose,
"I've got a secret that nobody knows!"
With petals so bright and a bold little sway,
She confessed to the weeds, it's a funny way.

"My colors are wild, but I'm shy on the side,
I tried to be bold, but oh, I would hide!"
The daisies all laughed, as they pranced about,
"You're our wild queen, without a doubt!"

Then each little bloom shared their odd little quirks,
A daffodil said, "I trip when it lurks!"
The poppies erupted, in laughter they rolled,
As petals exchanged stories, both funny and bold.

So remember, dear blooms, we each have our tales,
Just laugh at the quirks, and let laughter prevail,
For in the wild field, there's joy to unfold,
A patch of bright blossoms, with secrets untold.

Shadows of the Springtime Bloom

In the springtime, blooms took their turn,
With shadows that danced, eager to burn,
A lilac whispered, "I'm shy, can you tell?"
As dandelions giggled, "Oh, do really dwell!"

Petals in sunlight, they frolicked with glee,
Each color a joke, as bright as can be,
A tulip was prancing, quite full of itself,
While daisies declared, "Get off the shelf!"

The butterfly tiptoed, trying to act cool,
"I'm the best dancer in this blooming school!"
But the shadows just chuckled, they found it absurd,
As wind carried laughter, through every word.

So if you find blooms in their whimsical light,
Join in their folly, it feels just right,
For springtime's a stage, with blooms set to play,
Where laughter and joy dance the clouds away!

The Clover's Blessing

In the meadow, clovers play,
Hiding wishes, here they lay.
Lucky charms, green hats on heads,
Whispering secrets to drowsy beds.

Ants march proudly, parade in line,
Stealing crumbs, they think it's fine.
Grasshoppers sing a silly tune,
Grooving under the watchful moon.

Mice tell tales of the chef's delight,
Cooking cheese all through the night.
While daisies giggle, heads held high,
Join the fun as rabbits fly.

In this patch, all finds a friend,
Where laughter grows, there's no end.
Clover's blessing, a quirky gift,
In each petal, the spirits lift.

Illuminated by Marigold Light

Marigolds glow, a golden cheer,
They wink at bees that come quite near.
With every buzz, a dance begins,
Nature's jesters, adorned like kings.

Frogs jump high to catch a glimpse,
Of petals dressed in sunny trims.
They croak their jokes with silly flair,
While ladybugs twirl in mid-air.

Caterpillars wear tiny hats,
Debating over snacks like diplomats.
What's tastier, leaf or freeze-dried?
With every bite, another side.

In this theater of green and gold,
The merry blooms, brave and bold.
Beneath the glow, laughter takes flight,
All enchanting, in marigold light.

The Realm of the Peony

Peonies blush in shades divine,
With frilly skirts, they sip on wine.
They gossip softly about the breeze,
And giggle at the loyal bees.

Bumblebees wear polka-dot shoes,
Strutting around, they'll never lose.
While petals dance and twirl away,
In this garden, it's all play.

The snails slide down, so very slow,
Wearing shells like hats, what a show!
They refuse to race; they take their time,
In a realm where nothing's a crime.

Amid the blooms, the laughter swells,
Tales unfold, as the magic tells.
In the peony fields, joy is free,
A frolicsome world, come join with me.

Ferns and Fragments of Time

Ferns unfurl like jokes untold,
In shadows cool, they brave the bold.
They tickle footfalls, soft and light,
As tiny fairies take to flight.

Mushrooms pop up with tiny grins,
Sharing tales of all their sins.
They charm the squirrels with their caper,
A forest party with no paper.

Each leaf a whisper of days gone by,
When trees held secrets, reaching high.
Laughter lingers in the damp air,
Where mischief hides without a care.

Time meanders, wearing a smile,
Through paths of green, at its own style.
In this realm of ferns and rhymes,
Life's a laughter, across all times.

Memory of the Lavender Breeze

In fields where purple dreams are spun,
Bees buzz around, oh what fun!
A lavender breeze whispers with glee,
Tickling the noses of folks like me.

The rabbits dance, they think it's a show,
Pollen party, with much ado,
Wearing crowns of petals, they prance and play,
In this fragrant world, they just won't stay.

But oh the smell, it gets too strong,
A sneeze erupts, oh what's wrong?
The flowers giggle, they drop their rhyme,
As they watch us laugh in broken time.

So here's to breezes, so silly and bright,
Carrying scents that dance in the light,
In our lavender dreams, all worries cease,
Don't mind the rabbits; just laugh with ease!

The Petal Paperweight

A flower laid, so proud, so bold,
In the sun, it glimmers like gold,
But watch out! It's a petal's fate,
To nudge the paperweights straight out of date.

The breeze comes by, it sweeps them away,
Scattering stories of yesterday,
Who knew a daisy could take flight,
Making the office feel so light?

In a world of seriousness, it brings a grin,
As paper flies fast, oh where to begin?
Office pranks brought by a tulip's glow,
This paperweight's funny, it's quite the show!

So here's to petals that take to the air,
In meetings and memos, with flair to spare,
Let's laugh at the chaos their freedom creates,
As we chase after notes and fateful dates.

Songs of the Wisteria

Wisteria hangs, a curtain of fun,
Swaying and singing under the sun,
A rapper in bloom, it rhymes with the breeze,
Jiving and jiggling with whimsical ease.

The squirrels join in with their acorn beats,
While birds toss confetti with cheerful tweets,
Each petal a note in our silly refrain,
Who needs a concert? Just dance in the rain!

But oh, watch the vines when they get too tight,
They'll tie up your shoelaces, what a sight!
As laughter erupts from the blossoms' flair,
The songs of the wisteria fill up the air.

So here we are, with smiles wide and bright,
In gardens of giggles, where joy takes flight,
Let's waltz with blooming, our hearts all aglow,
In the zany rhythms of nature's own show!

Fragrance of Forgotten Memories

In moments of laughter, we stumble and sway,
Scent of the past shows us the way,
A whiff of nostalgia, it floats like a kite,
Reminding us of when we danced in delight.

The daisies chatter, "Do you remember when?"
We fell in the mud, oh where have those days been?
With every faint whiff, we chuckle and sigh,
As the blooms share secrets, beneath the blue sky.

A bouquet of mishaps, all wrapped in glee,
The fragrance of laughter is wild, oh so free,
Sprinkled with petals from stories long gone,
A sweet serenade of what we had drawn.

So let's gather petals that tell our old tales,
With winks and nods, like mischievous snails,
In the scent of the past, we find our delight,
As we bask in the joy of our whimsical plight.

The Comet's Blooming Journey

A comet streaks across the sky,
It leaves behind a flower high.
With petals bright in vibrant hues,
It tickles bees and pants their shoes.

The wind then laughs, a chuckle loud,
As skies burst forth with blooming cloud.
The daisies dance, they twist and twirl,
While butterflies begin to whirl.

Stars envy blooms, they shine so meek,
In gardens where the fairies sneak.
Each blossom hops, a joyful game,
While the comet's trail ignites a flame.

A giggle here, a giggle there,
The flowers play with sunlit air.
In this parade of silly cheer,
Who knew a comet could bring such glee here?

Nature's Silent Serenade

In silent woods, the flowers chat,
About the squirrel and his hat.
They gossip soft, in whispers clear,
Of nightly feasts and beetles' beers.

The trees lean close to catch the fun,
As daisies prank old Mr. Sun.
They lure him near, then hide away,
His blush ignites the break of day.

The butterflies take center stage,
With juggling acts that steal the page.
While willows sway and chuckle low,
They scoop up petals, steal the show.

Thus nature sings in quirky rhyme,
With laughter echoing through time.
In this sweet hum, the day does sway,
A symphony of blooms at play.

Harmonies of the Olive Branch

An olive tree strummed softly low,
In breezes where the daisies glow.
With leaves like fingers, strum a tune,
The flowers sway beneath the moon.

The bumblebees do jazz up tight,
While dandelions take to flight.
They spin and twirl in sun's embrace,
Chasing shadows with a laugh on their face.

Olives wink with glossy eyes,
As violets craft their sweet disguise.
The sweet aromas drift and sway,
Inviting all to join the play.

So gather round, both big and small,
For nature's tunes enchant us all.
In this grove, the joy expands,
As laughter blooms across the lands.

The Magic of Dandelion Wishes

A dandelion stands with flair,
Hats off to wishes in the air.
With tiny seeds that float and fly,
They giggle softly as they sigh.

Each puff releases dreams anew,
As children giggle, chasing too.
The race begins, they dash and run,
To catch the wishes, oh what fun!

Whispers last upon the breeze,
While flowers plot their tricks with ease.
They scatter seeds in cheeky prance,
Ensuring every child's chance.

So toss a wish and watch it soar,
On dandelion flights galore.
With every laugh and joyous scene,
The magic blooms in vibrant green.

Journey Through the Petal Maze

In a garden where daisies dance,
A bee thinks he's found romance.
He buzzes loud, making quite a fuss,
While butterflies giggle, oh what a fuss!

Roses giggle with a touch of flair,
They gossip about the tulips' hair.
A daffodil trips on a fancy leaf,
Causing the lilies to roar with disbelief!

Sunflowers turn their heads with glee,
Watching all the antics, oh look at me!
Pansies chuckle at a stubborn sprout,
Who tries to shout but can't get out!

A dandelion wishes with all its might,
To float away like a featherlight kite.
Yet stuck in the ground, it turns to cheer,
Laughing with friends, spreading joy and beer!

Reverie of the Wildflower Heart

In a meadow filled with wildflower dreams,
Butterflies plot their pranks and schemes.
A clumsy bumblebee trips on a vine,
But rolls with laughter, oh isn't he fine?

Poppies flirt with each passing cloud,
While daisies brag, feeling quite proud.
A daffy dandelion dares to declare,
"I'll be a wish, if you just blow air!"

The violets tell stories of whimsical tales,
Of rain and sunshine, and countless snails.
Midnight blooms giggle under the moon,
While crickets sing a lively tune!

Each petal's a joke, each leaf a jest,
In this garden of laughter, we're truly blessed.
With wildflowers giggling, it's clear to see,
Nature's humor thrives in wild jubilee!

Petals of Whispered Dreams

In the shade of a tulip's wide embrace,
All the flowers gather for a race.
But the prize? A sunbeam, bright and sweet,
Causing each bloom to shuffle on feet!

Lilies twist as they try to run,
While daisies giggle, "This is such fun!"
A sunflower shouts, "I'm winning for sure!"
But a passing breeze says, "You're just a bore!"

The violets tangle with ivy's long grip,
As pansies frown, they can't take a trip.
Yet all in good nature, they laugh and play,
Whispering dreams in the sun's warm ray.

When twilight falls, with stars up high,
The petals recall their fun-filled sky.
In a world of giggles, together they beam,
Swaying softly in the breeze like a dream!

The Language of Blossoms

In the corner of a garden wide,
Petals chatter in colors, bright and spry.
A tulip speaks in shades so grand,
While daisies tease, "We rule this land!"

"Listen closely, I tell you flat,
A hungry critter just ate my hat!"
Said a sunflower tall, with a nod so proud,
As a ladybug laughed, hiding in a shroud.

With petals speaking in whispers soft,
A pansy grinned, "I'm so far off!"
While the violets winked, playing a tune,
All under the watchful eye of the moon.

As night unfolds, the whispers glow,
Each petal a secret, a tale, a show.
In the garden's heart, where laughter hums,
The language of blossoms speaks joy, not glums!

Woven Threads of Color

In a meadow where daisies tease,
Buttercups laugh in the gentle breeze.
Tulips frolic with giggles bright,
While violets whisper, 'Is this the right height?'

Sunflowers stretch, trying to brag,
But the lilacs just roll and lag.
Their stories twirl like ribbons in air,
Each petal a secret, bold and rare.

The poppies dance in polka-dots,
While the roses play tricks, tying knots.
With every bloom, a tale unfolds,
In this garden where mischief holds.

So come here, where colors meet,
Join the blooms in their playful feat.
Laugh and cheer, let your worries slide,
In this patch where joy can't hide.

Garden of Forgotten Tales

Once there stood a grand old fern,
With stories lost, waiting for a turn.
A busy bee buzzed by in jest,
Said, 'Tell me quick, I need a rest!'

The marigolds whispered of yesteryears,
While the sage laughed through all his tears.
Dandelions snapped, 'We have more fun!'
But the violets just rolled in the sun.

Each petal holds a silly rhyme,
Woven in the fabric of time.
As the sun sets, they code a plan,
To giggle and wiggle, as best they can.

So if you stroll through blooms so bright,
Hear laughter ringing through the night.
In this garden where stories lie,
The flowers dance, and the world is spry.

The Orchid's Silent Song

An orchid stood, wearing a grin,
With petals bright, a whimsical spin.
She whispered to bees, 'Come join the fun!'
But they just buzzed, and away they run.

With a huff, she tried a little dance,
But stumbled on roots, missed her chance.
Grumpy old cacti rolled their eyes,
'With feet like those, no surprise!'

Yet she twinkled under bright sun beams,
Dreaming of wild and silly themes.
In her pot, she spun with glee,
Creating tales of absurdity.

So next time you're under that leafy shade,
Listen to her, don't be afraid.
For blooms can sing in colors rare,
With laughter they gift, floating in air.

Narrative of the Nightshade

In the dim light of the evening bloom,
Nightshade chuckled, dispelling gloom.
'What secrets hide in shadows deep?'
Asked the moon with a playful peep.

'Oh, I've tales of mischief untold,
Of hedgehogs and mice, oh so bold.
Once a squirrel wore a flower crown,
And danced through the night without a frown.'

The toadstool chimed in, quite loud,
'He slid on dew and thought he was proud!
But tripped on a twig, oh what a sight,
He landed right where the sun shines bright!'

The laughter echoed in the dark,
As nightshade spun each cheeky spark.
In moonlit tales, we find our way,
Where every flower has something to say.

Whispers of Petal Dreams

In a garden where daisies play,
Bumblebees dance in a silly way.
They buzz and hum, what a loud cheer!
The flowers giggle, 'Oh dear, oh dear!'

A bloom with stripes in colors bright,
Said, "I'm a zebra!" in the sunlight.
Tulips snickered, "Oh, what a sight!"
As petals twirled with sheer delight.

A rose wore glasses, quite the trend,
It whispered jokes to its leafy friend.
The lilies laughed, "We're not so keen,
On your fashion - a floral scene!"

Dandelions blew a wish or two,
Spreading laughter with the morning dew.
Their wishes tangled in the breeze,
And tickled the flowers with such ease.

The Garden's Secret Song

In the garden, a secret choir,
Sang to the sun with all desire.
They harmonized with funny rhymes,
Tickling bees in busy times.

A daffodil jumped, full of flair,
"Look at me! I'm a millionaire!"
Petunias rolled their eyes and said,
"Not with roots stuck in the bed!"

A sunflower stood, tried to rap,
"Yo, I'm tall! Look at my map!"
But daisies giggled soft and bright,
"Your skills need more than just sunlight!"

In shadows where the critters roam,
They whispered tunes of garden gnome.
With quirky notes and silly cheer,
The flowers danced, the bugs drew near.

Tales Beneath the Blossoms

Beneath the blossoms, secrets hide,
Where ants march on their silly glide.
A petal dreams of a grand parade,
While roses plot a joke to trade.

A buttercup claimed it had a crown,
While violets laughed, "You're just a clown!"
Hibiscus whispered with a grin,
"I flower bright, but spin to win!"

A wily worm told tales of old,
Of flowers bold who turned to gold.
The pansies giggled, "We like fun,
But golden flowers? They're on the run!"

Clay pots chuckled, gossip to share,
"Did you see that bloom with purple hair?"
The garden thrummed with laughter's song,
Where all the plants just bloom along.

Secrets in the Flowerbed

In a flowerbed, where secrets lie,
Petals whisper, passing by.
A sleepy bee in a bright blue hat,
Said, "I'm the king of this habitat!"

A daisy sighed, "That's quite absurd,
You're just a buzz in the morning herd!"
Lilies peeked from behind a bush,
And said, "Too much chatter makes us hush!"

A sunflower claimed it lost its way,
While buttercups giggled, "Here, come play!"
They spun in circles, a dizzy crew,
Telling tales that nobody knew.

With secrets shared and laughter bright,
The flowerbed bloomed from day to night.
In every petal, a story spun,
Of funny blooms, just having fun!

The Tulip's Tale of Love

In a garden bright and gay,
A tulip sought a date to play.
She wore her petals, red and fine,
But tripped on roots and spilled her wine.

The daffodils all laughed aloud,
As she fell face-first, feeling proud.
Yet love, it bloomed in disarray,
For bloopers often lead to sway.

A bumblebee buzzed by her side,
Said, "Goodness, love, you have some pride!"
With a wiggle, she caught his glance,
Together they began to dance.

So tulips, take a lesson here,
Love might bloom when you trip, my dear.
A stumble here, a giggle there,
Two hearts in laughter, what a pair!

Sonnet to the Sunflower

Oh, sunflower, you tower so high,
With your golden face, you touch the sky.
Yet in your stalk, a secret's told,
Of squirrels who raid your seeds of gold.

You sway and smile, so proud you stand,
While chipmunks form a sneaky band.
They nibble bits and giggle bright,
As you just bask in morning light.

But when you turn to follow the sun,
Those rascals think they've won the fun.
Oh, dear sunflower, what a sight,
A heist beneath your blooms so bright!

So when you shine, just let it be,
A merry game of hide and glee.
Though seeds may vanish in the breeze,
Your charming face is sure to please!

The Camellia's Secret

The camellia sat with a sigh,
Pondering why her petals shied.
"Why not flaunt your lovely hue?"
The gardener asked, with laughter too.

With a laugh, she told a tale,
Of how she often would regale.
Each bud she wore was dressed in fluff,
Yet she felt, sometimes, it was too much.

"If I flaunt too much, will they all gawk?
Or applaud my charm, and giddy squawk?"
The blooms beside her tried to reassure,
"Dear camellia, be bright and pure!"

So on a whim, she took the stage,
Danced and twirled, a flowery rage.
Now she glows with all her might,
And giggles loud with pure delight!

Journey Through the Herbarium

A ladybug packed for a trip,
Through the herbarium, she'd skip.
With mint and sage in her tiny bag,
She thought of all the fun to brag.

She bumbled past the basil crowd,
Their scent so strong, they felt so proud.
"Hey, ladybug, you smell so sweet!
Join us for a fragrant feat!"

Then came a whiff of rosemary,
"Care to add some spice, dear fairy?"
They danced upon the verdant floor,
With salads served, they wanted more!

But by the thyme, she lost her way,
In minty dreams, she lost the day.
Through laughter, herbs, and sprightly cheer,
A ladybug found friends so dear!

Sagas of the Wilted Stem

In a garden where daisies tell tales,
The roses wear socks and a hint of old pales.
A sunflower dances, with wobbling feet,
While the weeds share gossip, what a funny treat!

A cactus tried jumping, but landed on air,
The tulips are laughing, with petals to spare.
A beetle named Bob thought he could compete,
But tripped on a daisy, what a silly feat!

The daisies still giggle as night starts to creep,
While the fruit trees take wee little naps, oh so deep.
A bumblebee jives with a hum and a flutter,
He stings with sweet laughter, not a worry to utter!

Thus the garden grows wilder, a whimsical dream,
From the tales of the flowers, the ruckus, the gleam.
With stories of laughter, all day long spun,
In the heart of the wild, where spirits are fun!

The Beauty in Decay

Once a sunflower basked in golden delight,
But drooped with a sigh in the fading moonlight.
Its petals fell off, like a hat, such a show,
Yet laughed with the breeze, 'I still steal the glow!'

The garden said, 'Look, how lovely you wear,
A crown made of rust, with some vintage flair!'
The leaves joined in chorus, a rustling spree,
'In decay lies the beauty, come dance with me!'

A wilted rose joked about growing some thorns,
While the daisies shared tales of weathered morns.
The earth chuckled softly, holding secrets untold,
In every brown spot, a treasure to behold!

So let not the wilting bring grief to your heart,
For beauty's a puzzle, a curious art.
In each fading petal, a whisper's embrace,
A giggle from nature, a grand open space!

Sunflowers at Dusk

In a field of sunflowers, they wink at the sun,
With faces so sunny, they're having such fun.
The evening descends, as the sky turns to gold,
Those cheeky blooms chatter, their stories unfold.

They all share a secret, 'till night does arrive,
That scaring the moon is their plan to survive.
With a flap and a giggle, they sway with the breeze,
The starlight comes out for a moment of tease.

But the moon rolls her eyes, 'Oh what a bright crew!
To think they can outshine the soft glow of blue!'
Yet the sunflowers cheer, with laughter and cheer,
Gather round, dear night, for we hold no fear!

As dusk wraps the world in a whimsical cloak,
These sun-drenched jesters, they dance, and they poke.
In nature's own theater, a joyous display,
The sunflowers at dusk keep the worries at bay!

The Velvet Shadows of Flora

In the velvet shadows where blossoms reside,
The lilies conspire, with giggles inside.
The violets plot pranks, while the daisies, so spry,
Chase butterflies gleefully, up in the sky.

The tulips declare, 'This is pranking brigade!'
Under stars, they giggle, in laughter they fade.
With whispers of mischief, they sneak and they play,
Each flower a player in this whimsical ballet.

A comical cactus, dressed up for the night,
Wears a tutu of thorns, oh what a sight!
The roses all swoon at his quirky parade,
A king of the garden, this prince of the shade!

As moonlight bathes blooms in a silvery hue,
The laughter of petals reveals something new.
In shadows of flora, under bright twinkling stars,
The joy of their antics transcends all the scars!

Chronicles of the Twining Vines

Two vines held hands, a tangled spree,
Their leafy dance was quite a sight to see.
One whispered jokes, the other just sighed,
"We're just vine, let's take this ride!"

They climbed a fence, but slid right down,
Laughing at how they formed a crown.
"Let's plant some seeds to spread more cheer,
Or risk a realm of weeds, I fear!"

Up in the sky, a butterfly scoffed,
"A tangled mess of green, you're soft!"
But down below, the roots took hold,
Making a tale that's fun and bold!

The sun peeped in, winking with glee,
"This leafy circus is fun for me!"
So twine away, dear friend of trees,
Life is a joke, spread joy with ease!

Sunlight's Gentle Brush

Morning rays tickle the daisies' heads,
While bees wear crowns of dew-soaked threads.
Sunshine laughed, while flowers swayed,
"Hey! You missed a spot!" it playfully played.

A petal flicked, and a bug fell off,
"Did you hear that? Was that a scoff?"
The daisies giggled, blushing so bright,
While the sun just grinned, a pure delight!

"Don't forget to shine, oh foliage crew,"
Sunlight chirped, "I'll brush you too!"
With each soft sweep, the garden awoke,
Who would've thought sunshine could joke?

So dance under solar glow, dear blooms,
Chase away shadows, erase the glooms!
A giggle from nature brings laughter near,
In this sun-kissed kingdom, we cheer!

The Tale of Two Petals

Two petals met on a windy day,
"What's your plan? Let's frolic and play!"
One said, "I'll twirl; you catch the breeze,"
They spun around like carefree tease.

The first one boasted, "I'm a color rare!"
But then a bug shouted, "You're full of air!"
With laughter shared, they lost their style,
And rolled on the grass for quite a while.

A ladybug laughed, "You're a fragrant pair,
But can you dance? It's time to dare!"
They tried a jig, but flopped like fools,
Planting themselves in mud, oh dear, no jewels!

In the end, they giggled, muddy and bright,
"Let's stick together; it feels just right!"
Two petals united, laughter their bond,
Creating a tale, just like a fond!

Gossamer Dreams in Green

Once in a meadow, a dream took flight,
With dandelions laughing, oh what a sight!
A wish floated by, riding on a breeze,
Said, "Catch me if you can, I'll tease!"

A frog in a pond sang, "What's that I see?
A wisp of a dream that's not meant for me!"
He leaped with joy but landed with a splat,
"Better luck next time, how 'bout that?"

The flowers joined in, spinning tales so bright,
"Let's turn this meadow into a starry night!"
With giggles and whispers, they formed a swirl,
In gossamer laughter, they began to twirl.

So here in the meadow, where dreams take rest,
Every petal chuckles, feeling quite blessed.
For laughter is magic, blooming so free,
In a world where fun thrives, we all agree!

A Symphony of Petals

In a garden, petals dance,
They twirl and swirl, given a chance.
A daisy trips, a rose lets out a giggle,
The whole bouquet begins to wiggle.

Lilies laugh with leaves in tow,
Jasmine jokes, 'Here comes the show!'
Sunflowers burst with sunny cheer,
"I'll stand tall!" they shout, "Never fear!"

Tulips tease with bright, wild flair,
"Watch out for bees, they'll steal your hair!"
With every breeze, the petals sway,
A symphony blooms, what a display!

In this patch of jest and shine,
Nature's laughter is truly divine.
Join the giggle, let worries cease,
In this floral fiesta, find your peace.

The Dandelion's Journey

A dandelion puffed with pride,
Set off on a journey, ready to ride.
Blown by the wind, it called, "Whee!"
Floating off, as happy as can be.

Through fields of dreams and skies so blue,
It tickled the clouds, like feathers it flew.
"Look at me!" it shouted with glee,
As butterflies danced and bees sang free.

It landed in puddles, and splashed with delight,
"I'm not just a weed! I shine oh so bright!"
With seeds in a chorus, they giggled and played,
Each one a wish, in the sun's gentle shade.

So here's to the wishes, so light and so bold,
The dandelion's tale, forever retold.
With laughter and joy, let your wishes take flight,
In the whimsical breeze of a summer night.

Fables of the Wildflower

In the meadow where wildflowers grow,
A tale of mischief, it starts to flow.
The poppies plotted, so clever and spry,
To prank the sun with a capricious sigh.

They whispered, "Let's play hide and seek,
While sunbeams dance, just hide, don't peek!"
The daisies chuckled, the violets agreed,
A game unfurled, wild laughter freed.

Butterflies joined in, fluttering near,
"We'll be the judges, let's bring some cheer!"
As blooms hid their faces and giggled in glee,
All nature erupted with whimsical spree.

But the sun caught on, with a chuckle and grin,
"I'll find you all, just wait, let the fun begin!"
With petals in laughter, the meadow was bright,
The fables of wildflowers brought pure delight.

Shadows of the Bamboo Grove

In shadows where bamboo stands so tall,
A quirky tale of laughter does call.
Leaves tickle softly in the breeze,
As pandas giggle and beg for peas.

The stalks sway gently, sharing their jokes,
While monkeys swing, playing pranks on folks.
"Hey, did you hear the one with the breeze?"
"Mmm, was that a joke or just rusting leaves?"

Together they conspire, a mischievous lot,
"Let's see who falls for the silliest plot!"
A whisper of wind, a tumble, a roll,
Bamboo giggles echo, that's how they stroll.

In the grove where shadows endlessly play,
Nature's own jesters brighten the day.
So join in the laughter, embrace every move,
In this bamboo ballet, find your groove.

A Tapestry of Garden Stories

In a garden wide and bright,
A gnome tripped in broad daylight.
He knocked over daisies, what a sight!
The flowers giggled with pure delight.

A rose with a wink said, "Not so fast!"
While tulips sang their tune, steadfast.
A snail raced by, but never last,
In this lush world, everyone's a blast.

The violets played hide and seek,
While sunflowers danced to a beat so sleek.
A bee buzzed by, quite the peak,
Telling jokes, making laughter unique.

In this patch of color, stories unfold,
Of antics and mischief, brave and bold.
Every petal has a tale to be told,
In a tapestry of joy, never cold.

The Pollen Path

On a path paved with pollen gold,
Bees hold court, their tales unfold.
One wore glasses, not very bold,
Said, "Life's sweet! Just look, behold!"

A butterfly flitted, flapping wings,
Claiming to know all the best things.
"Try this flower!" oh, the joy it brings,
With laughter and nectar, the garden sings.

A ladybug joined with a tiny cheer,
"Let's dance on petals, oh my dear!"
The ants marched by, without a fear,
Making maps while they sipped their beer.

As moonlight washed the blooms in fun,
The creatures frolicked, all as one.
In the garden, laughter had just begun,
Life's a festival, or so it's spun.

Sweet-Nectar Chronicles

In a cool breeze filled with glee,
A bee said, "Why bother to flee?"
"When nectar flows, just let it be!"
With a chuckle, he swam in wild tea.

Beneath the blooms, a squirrel danced,
Accidentally, he found romance.
With petals like skirts in a colorful prance,
He twirled and swayed, lost in chance.

A hummingbird hovered, what a sight!
She sipped and giggled, pure delight.
"With every drop, I take flight!"
The garden glowed, all sparkly and bright.

In tales of sweet nectar to share,
The blooms join in with laughter rare.
Every sip, a story laid bare,
In this place, not a single care.

The Hidden Language of Lilies

At midnight, lilies start to chat,
With gossip that's funny, imagine that!
One said, "Have you seen the old cat?"
The others giggled, oh, where's he at?

A daisy chimed in with a grin,
"He thinks he's a lion, oh what a spin!"
With petals all perky, the laughter did win,
In the moonlit garden, joy did begin.

The lilies swayed, with jokes to share,
About bees in tuxedos, and pants that aren't rare.
"Why dress so fancy?" said one with flair,
"Nectar is calling, without a care!"

In whispers of petals, secrets flow,
Of ball gowns and humor, a captivating show.
The night blooms with stories, don't you know?
In their hidden language, laughter does grow.

Whimsy in the Whispering Thicket

In the thicket, leaves conspire,
To tell tales of birds on wire.
A squirrel's dance, a flower's grin,
Who knew such chaos could begin?

Behind a bush, a gnome snores loud,
Dreaming of being in a crowd.
The daisies giggle, oh what a sight,
As dandelions take to flight!

A butterfly wearing a tiny hat,
Inspects the petals like a diplomat.
With every flutter and cheeky twirl,
He claims the garden, the king of the swirl!

Yet in this thicket, fun runs free,
With secrets whispered from tree to tree.
Laughter blooms at every turn,
As nature's jesters together churn.

The Garden of Time's Secrets

In the garden, the clock ticks slow,
Where daisies argue, and sunflowers glow.
A rabbit wearing spectacles reads,
The stories carried by the winds and seeds.

Time's secrets hidden in lily's plight,
A gossiping bee takes flight at night.
Flowers snicker as stories unfold,
Of petals lost and moments bold.

The gnarled oak grumbles in fun little rhymes,
While vines intertwine through curious times.
"It's my turn now," the tulip chimes,
"I swear I'm taller than last summer's climbs!"

Yet as hours pass in whimsical glee,
Past the petals, as far as can be,
The garden giggles, forever it seems,
Holding secrets whispered in dreams.

Reflections in a Rose's Dew

A drop of dew upon a petal bright,
Reflects a ladybug's surprising flight.
"Did you see that?" the blossoms coo,
As thorns gossip, sharing viewpoints anew.

A butterfly struts in glittering pride,
Casting shadows where the secrets hide.
"Look at me," he boasts, as bees roll their eyes,
"Your color's lovely, but look at my size!"

Petals blush in the morning's cheer,
As whispers tickle from ear to ear.
The sun chuckles at the garden's jest,
While flowers plan their vibrant quest.

Dew drops giggle, reflections in play,
Chasing the sunlight throughout the day.
In this blooming side of nature's law,
Joy flips and flutters, a vibrant saw.

The Enigma of the Chrysanthemum

Chrysanthemum, with petals so round,
Holds mysteries deep in the soil's profound.
"What's with the fuss?" she winks with flair,
"It's just a little drama unaware!"

Wise old ferns whisper gossip galore,
As butterflies twirl and giggle, implore.
"Do you think they know of our plot so sly?"
"Of course not! They're busy just passing by!"

A robin arrives with a wild hairdo,
"Fashion in flowers? Oh, what's new?"
As petals chatter over morning's brew,
Creating theories about the morning dew.

In this secret world, laughter reigns true,
Where petals and whispers share the view.
Chrysanthemum grins, with a wink and a laugh,
As the garden spins tales on its leafy path.

The Poppy's Requiem

In a field of red, the poppies prance,
They wore little hats, all set for a dance.
With a flap and a flutter, they twirled with glee,
But tripped on their petals, oh woe, not me!

One shouted to daisies, 'Come join our fun!'
They giggled at poppies, 'This looks like a pun!'
But a breeze swept through, and made quite a mess,
As pollen went flying, oh what a distress!

The sun dipped down low, as they rolled on the ground,
Stuck together in blooms, as the laughter resound.
But a cloud overhead, now that was the bay,
They soaked in the shower, and washed all the play!

So here's to the petals, those bright little sprites,
Who dance in the sunshine, and giggle at nights.
Their dash of delight, a sight to behold,
In a tapestry tangled, their stories unfold.

A Gentle Wind's Narrative

Whispers of breezes through gardens so grand,
Tickled the tulips, a quirky band.
They tossed their heads back, a sight quite absurd,
Spinning tales to each other, oh how they stirred!

The roses chimed in, with a wink and a sigh,
'We'll tell you a secret, if you'd like to pry!'
But the wind just chuckled, with a playful swoon,
'You petals are splendid, but silly as June!'

Then daisies made daisy chains, quite the charade,
While violets argued of how they were made.
'You think you're the brightest?' the marigolds scoffed,
As the sunlight played tag, and petals got soft!

Yet amidst all the laughter, bright colors abound,
The air filled with stories, in circles they wound.
A wind of amusement, with quips both loud and light,
In the garden of giggles, where joy took flight.

Aggregates of Aroma

In a meadow of scents, the flowers convene,
Jasmine barges in, 'I'm the freshest, you've seen!'
But lavender chuckles, 'Oh please hold your reign,
For when bees come buzzing, it's all in the game!'

Then peonies chimed in, with petals so bright,
'We're the life of the party, and we smell just right!'
With a sway and a nod, they each took their turn,
But daffodils shouted, 'It's my chance to burn!'

A riot of aromas, they jostled and danced,
While sunflowers smiled, with their heads all enhanced.
The scents mixed and mingled, grew sweeter by far,
As scents made a ruckus, like a car at a bazaar!

So they laughed and they played, until day turned to dusk,

In a whirlwind of fragrance, a magical husk.
For amidst all the banter, they knew what was true,
Together they blossomed, that much was their cue.

The Cosmos of Carnations

In the cosmos of blooms, the carnations do twirl,
With ruffles and swirls, like a dance party swirl.
They beeped and they booped, in bright colors they shone,

Each petal a story, a wonderfull tone!

With winks from the daisies, they spun through the air,
While the lilies just watched, with their usual flare.
A galaxy formed with a giggle and sway,
In this floral universe, where flowers play!

Carnations declared, 'What a sight, don't you see?
We'll form a new planet, just cozy and free!'
But the violets exclaimed, 'Oh wait, hold the phone!
Let's make it a club, where the laughter has grown!'

So they twirled and they twisted, till the day turned to night,
Creating constellations, now that's quite the sight!
In the cosmos of blooms, they lived hand in hand,
With petals all aglow, who could withstand?

The Gerbera's Gift

In a garden bright, a Gerbera cried,
"Please don't plant me with that cactus beside!"
"I might wilt and wither, oh what a fate!"
But the cactus just chuckled, "Oh, isn't it great?"

With colors so wild, the Gerbera pranced,
"I've got the moves, come join in this dance!"
The daisies all giggled, they couldn't resist,
As petals swayed gently, not a chance they'd missed.

"Why do bees buzz? It's quite hard to tell!"
The Gerbera pondered, then rang a bell.
"They're saying it's sweet! So let's have some fun,
A party with nectar? Oh boy, I have won!"

So with laughter and cheers, they filled up the air,
The Gerbera's gift was joy everywhere!
With flowers so bright and spirits so high,
Even the moon winked in the darkening sky.

Visions Among the Hibiscus

A hibiscus once dreamed of a fancy new hat,
"Adorned with some sequins, I'll surely look fat!"
But a friend whispered gently, "Darling, don't fret,
Your glory's in bloom, and you're quite a set!"

So off they went planning a garden soirée,
Inviting all flowers, come out to play!
The daisies wore bows, the roses dressed bold,
While the hibiscus shimmered like petals of gold.

The sun baked the earth, and the breeze had a laugh,
Each flower shared stories, like a botanical staff.
The orchids recited some comical verse,
While the marigolds danced, oh, it couldn't be worse!

Then a bug in a tuxedo came waltzing right by,
"Who invited this fellow? It's too bold to try!"
But the hibiscus just giggled, adorned with a grin,
"Let's see who can twirl, let the fun now begin!"

The Whispering Willow

The willow was known for its gossip, oh dear,
With branches that waved, it would lend you an ear.
"Have you heard about Daisy?" it whispered with glee,
"She danced with a bee, it's no joke, can't you see?"

Underneath its long limbs, the squirrels would scheme,
"We'll sneak to the pond, where the lilies all dream!"
But the willow just chuckled, "I've heard this before,
Still, a splash in the water sounds fun—let's explore!"

One day as they played, there came a loud thud,
A raccoon rolled in, all covered in mud!
"Is this how you party?" the still willow laughed,
With branches a-swaying, it wrote their next craft.

"It's raucous, it's messy, but oh what a sight!
We'll dance till the dawn, till we blend with the night!"
And under the stars, the whole garden was bright,
With laughter and joy, such a magical night.

Tales from the Secret Garden

In a secret spot where the wildflowers grew,
A violet once claimed, "I am sweet, yes it's true!"
But the tulip just snickered, "Don't boast so too loud,
I'm regal and stunning—let's make a crowd!"

They gathered the daisies and roses so pink,
To share all their stories, the thoughts they would think.
"Who tied the best bow, or sang such a tune?
Let's see who can shine under this glowing moon!"

A sunflower stood tall, with a crown on its head,
"Come hear my tall tales, or I'll fill you with dread!"
But the flowers just giggled, fearing no fright,
"Your stories are sweet; let's stay up all night!"

So under the stars, in the cool evening air,
They shared all their secrets, each flower laid bare.
And as dawn approached, with the sun's bright ascent,
They laughed at their tales, a moment well spent.

Echoes of Nature's Story

In the garden, bees start to dance,
Petals twirl in a sunny prance.
A squirrel mistook a daisy for cheese,
Chased by a rabbit with a wink and a tease.

The flowers gossip, oh what a scene,
'What's that smell? Is it beans or is it green?'
The daisies chuckle, the roses just sigh,
While tulips play tag, reaching for the sky.

A ladybug laughed at a caterpillar's plea,
'You'll spin into silk? Just wait and see!'
With every tickle, the blooms get a thrill,
Nature's own antics, a comedic spill.

As evening creeps in, the jokes still unfurl,
With crickets reciting their own little whirl.
Amidst all the giggles, the sun starts to drop,
In the garden of chuckles, the laughter won't stop.

Vignettes Among the Violets

Once there was a bee with an appetite grand,
Who mistook sweet nectar for cake in the sand.
The violets giggled, unable to stand,
As he danced in a circle, his plan unplanned.

A wise old snail told tales of the past,
'Count not on speed, for slow is a blast!'
The butterflies swooped, giving him a cheer,
'You're just as slow, but we love you dear!'

Amongst the violets, a warm breeze does flow,
A grasshopper croons, quite the primrose show.
He fluffs up his wings, singing high and aloof,
'This is my stage! Come, dance on the roof!'

With giggles and laughter, the night turns to fun,
The stars above wink, proud of what they've done.
In this patchwork of life, where jokes intertwine,
Among violets' hues, all bloom, laugh, and shine.

The Rose That Spoke

Once a rose with a voice so sweet,
Complained of her thorns as she spoke to a beet.
'Why can't I have petals that scatter and shine?
Instead, here I sit, with this prickly design!'

The beetle replied, winking so sly,
'Your thorns are your armor, they make you fly high!'
With laughter, the rose found her spirit reign,
'Who knew being prickly could bring such a gain?'

A bumblebee chimed in, buzzing with glee,
'Lady, your fragrance is just heavenly!'
But the rose, so sarcastic, just rolled her green eyes,
'Only if they could smell my love-struck sighs!'

At dusk she sang ballads to fireflies bright,
Her petals aglow in the softening light.
With a wink and a twirl, she embraced her retreat,
For the rose that spoke turned her thorns into sweet.

Sunlit Stories of the Meadow

In a meadow where daisies play tag with the breeze,
A butterfly tripped over clover with ease.
She landed on grass, spreading stories so loud,
The daisies broke into laughter, feeling so proud.

A chipmunk was bragging of nuts he had found,
But slipped on a flower, landing flat on the ground.
The blooms erupted in giggles and delight,
'That's what you get for such boasting tonight!'

The sunflowers sunbathed in afternoon rays,
While a lone tulip freestyled, with flair in her ways.
She twirled in her petals, made the bees swoon,
'Just call me the star, I'll bloom to my tune!'

As the sky turned to pink and the day wound down,
The laughter echoed, not a single frown.
In the sunlit meadow, where joy is the key,
Each flower finds fun in wild jubilee!

www.ingramcontent.com/pod-product-compliance
Lightning Source LLC
Chambersburg PA
CBHW072140200426
43209CB00051B/189